I'm Just Me

KENZI JUPP

Ilustration

JOHN SUTCLIFFE

As it's an invisible condition,

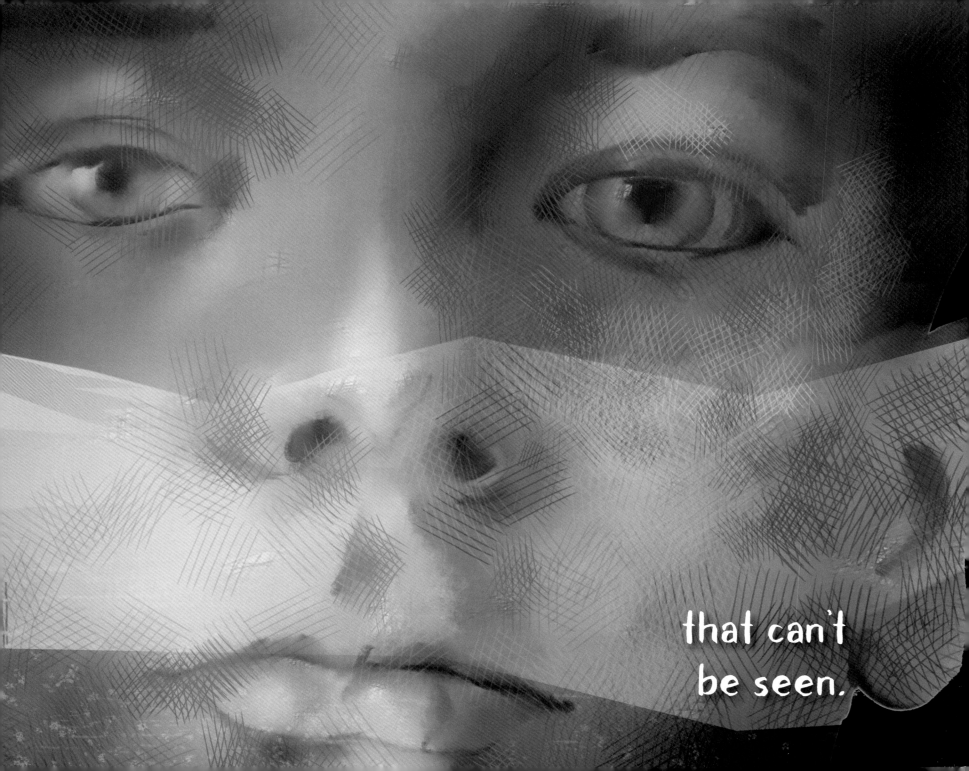

that can't
be seen.

when I run or walk.

So I'm autistic.

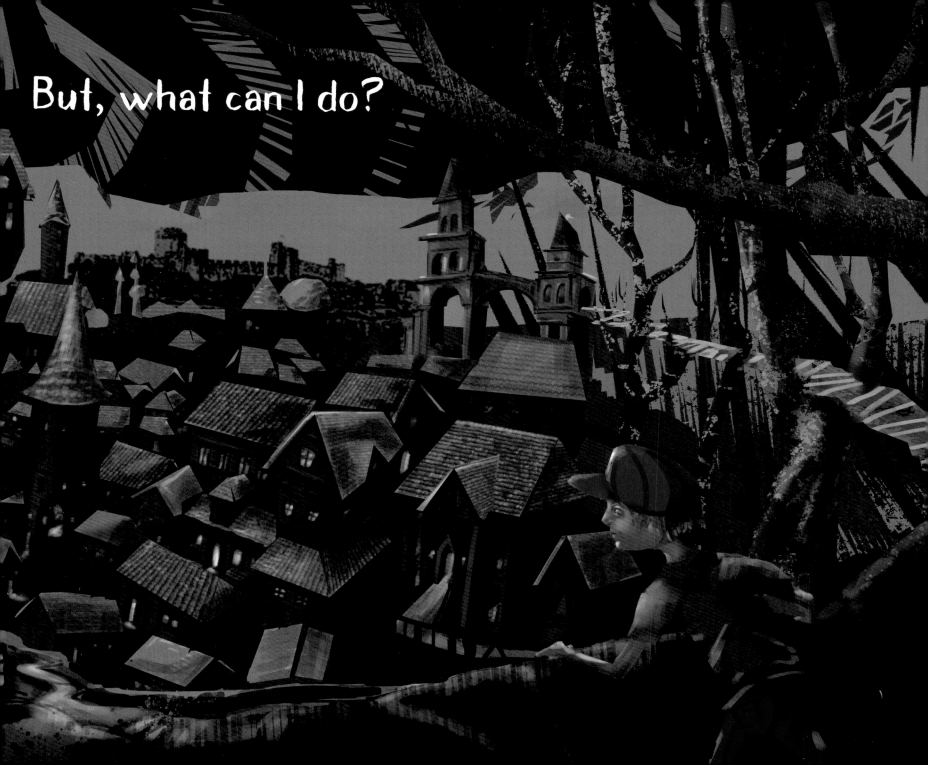

Virtually everything,

the same
as you.

at a different speed.

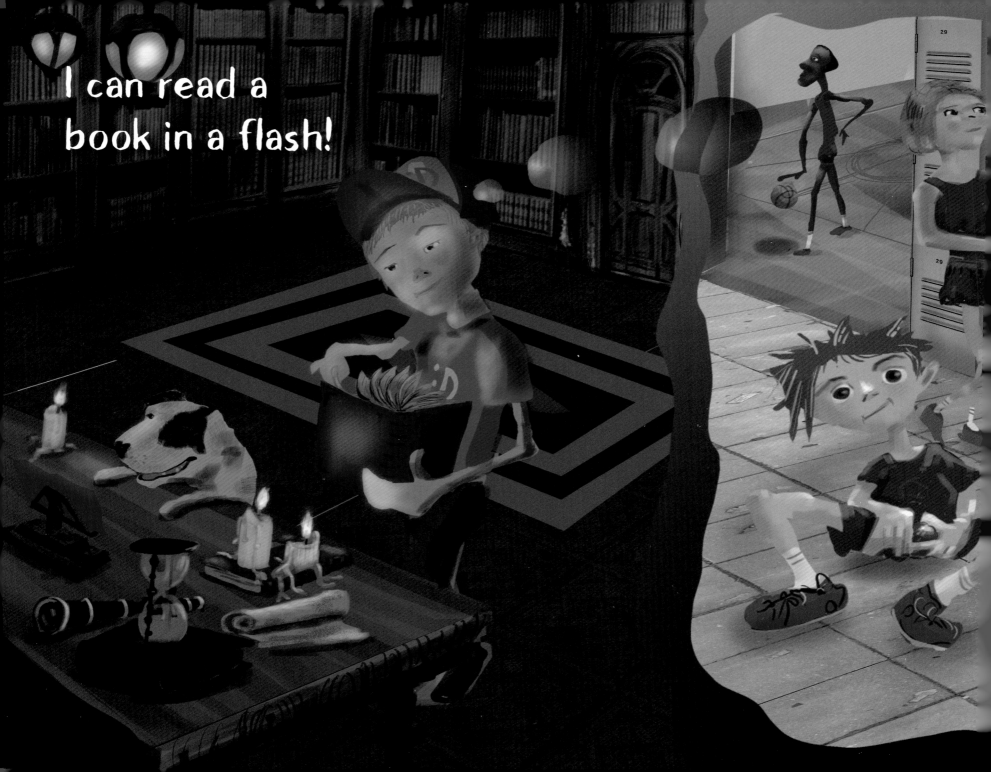

I can read a
book in a flash!

But, changing for P.E.?
It's extra time that I need.

But look back
in the books of history,

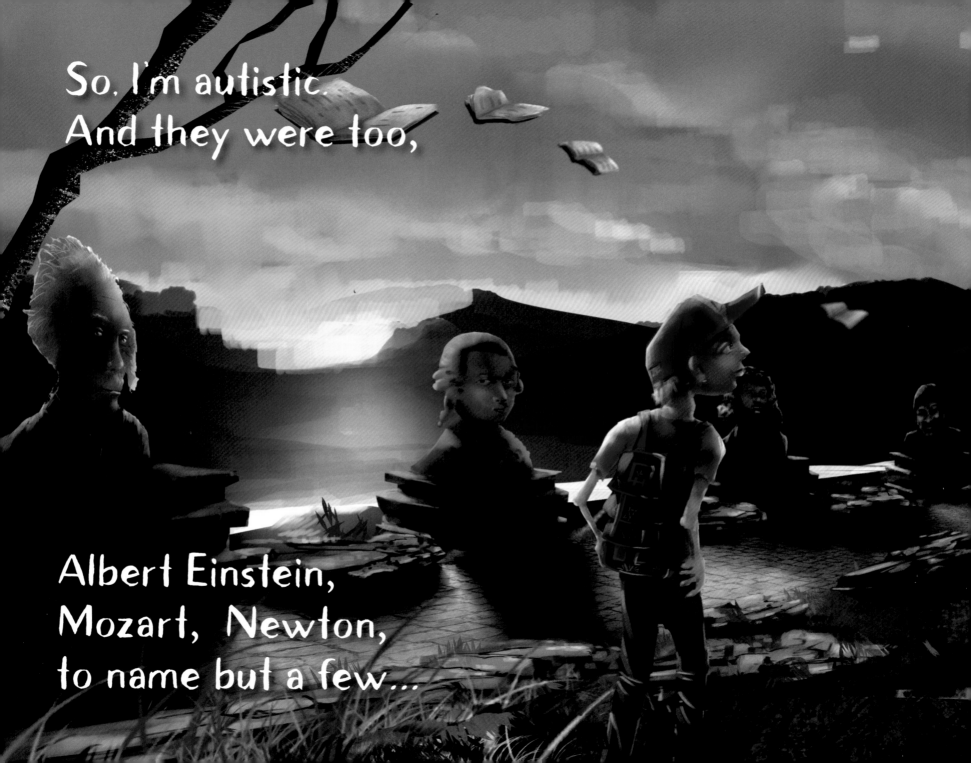

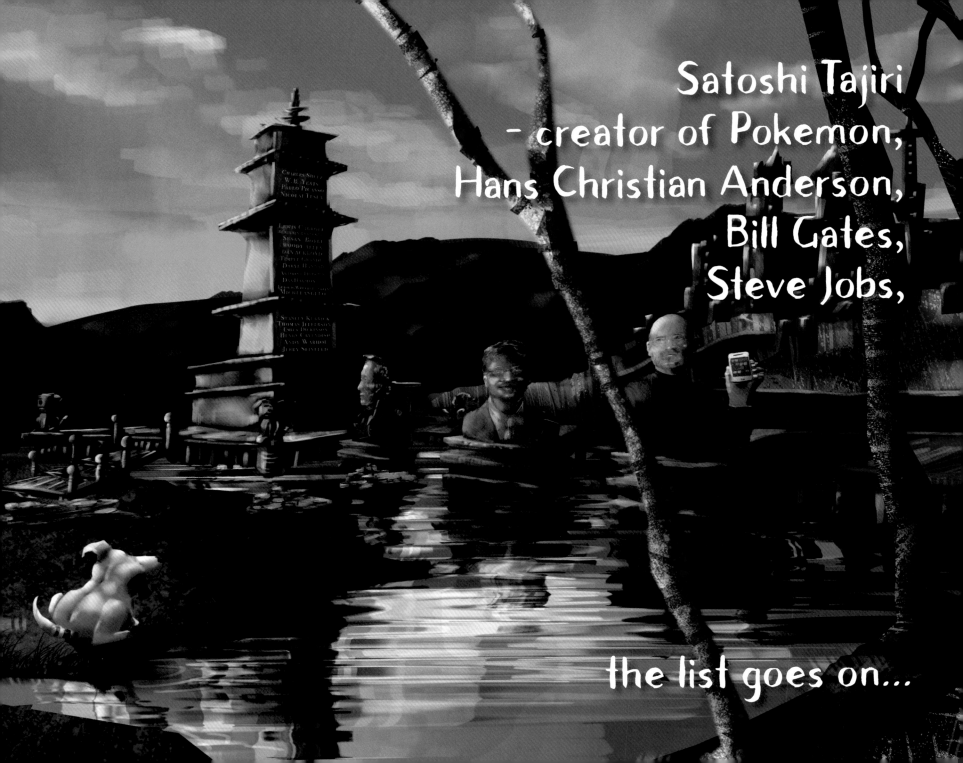

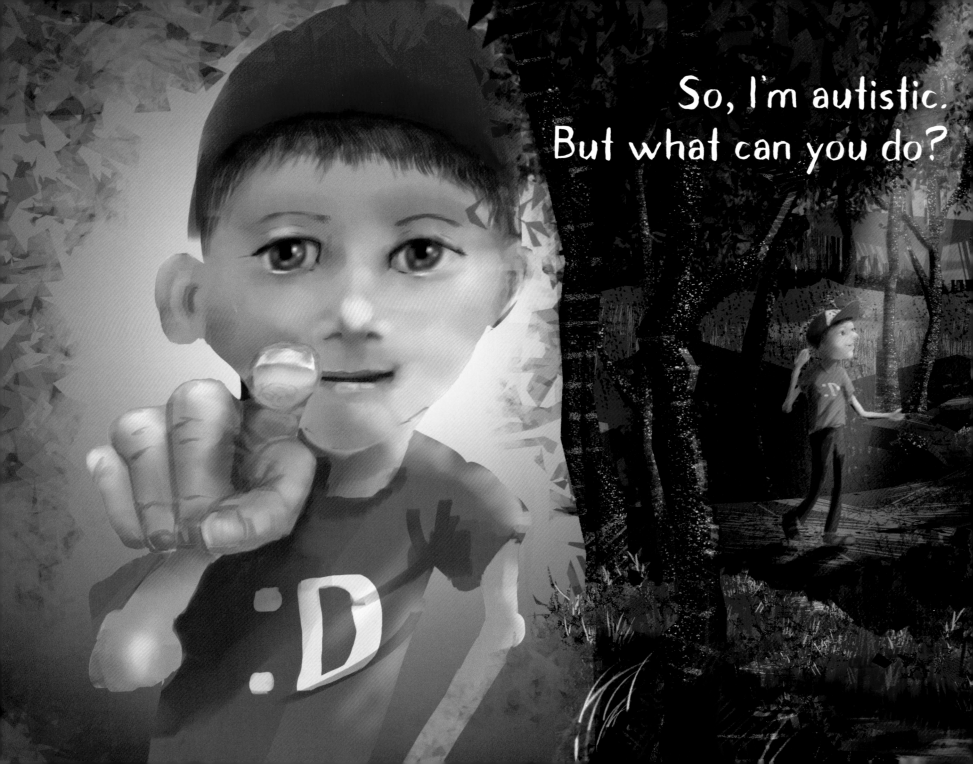

To help me be happy,
Like all of you..,

Talk to me.
Include me.